PUPIL
WORKBOOK
YEAR 6

Contents

Classification of living things

Evolution and inheritance

What light does

Human circulation

Electricity: changing circuits

Body health

Classification of living things

Lesson 1 How can we group living things?

Key vocabulary

Carl Linnaeus	fungi	kingdom	organism	taxonomy
classification	invertebrate	monera	protista	vertebrate

Activity 1: Classification

Read the text below about the scientist **Carl Linnaeus** and answer the questions.

Shown here as a statue in the Botanic Gardens (Botaniska Trädgården) in Gothenburg, Sweden, Carl Linnaeus is known as the Father of **Taxonomy**. This Swedish scientist, who was a botanist, zoologist, taxonomist and physician, developed his system of grouping (classifying) organisms based on what he could see and how living things were the same as or different from each other. This is known as taxonomy. We still use Linnaeus' taxonomy today, although there have been changes and modifications. Scientific advances and new evidence (particularly microscopic technology) have taught us more about the living world since the development of the original taxonomy.

Statue of Carl Linnaeus

Where was Carl Linnaeus from?

_____

What did Carl Linnaeus do?

_____

Why have classification and taxonomy changed since Linnaeus created his system?

_____

_____

_____

Look at this diagram. It shows the groups of living things. Talk to a partner about the groups.

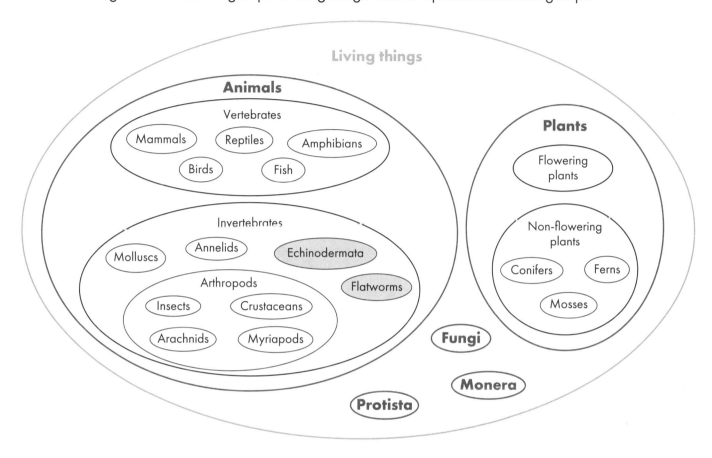

Write the name and group of four organisms you know. An organism is a living thing.

Organism: _____ Group: _____

Organism: _____ Group: _____

Organism: _____ Group: _____

Organism: _____ Group: _____

Are there any groups that you have not heard of before? Talk to a partner about what they might be. You will learn about them in this module.

Activity 3: Classifying living things

Write the name of each organism in the correct column of the table to show which group it belongs to.

chantelle mushroom

green algae

antra bacterium

natterjack toad

African elephant

common earthworm

brown centipede

runner bean

daffodil

water spider

Plant	Animal	Fungi	Protista (algae)	Monera (bacteria)

Activity 4: Identifying vertebrates and invertebrates

Animals can be grouped into two groups: animals that have a backbone and animals that do not. Vertebrates have an internal backbone, invertebrates do not.

Circle the invertebrates below.

| dolphin | ostrich | tortoise | beetle | mussel | slug |

Activity 5: Vertebrate characteristics

Vertebrates and invertebrates can be classified into smaller groups.

Vertebrates: **mammals**, **birds**, **reptiles**, **amphibians** and **fish**.

Invertebrates: **arthropods**, **molluscs**, **annelids**, **flatworms** and **echinodermata**.

The animals in each group share many similar characteristics. Identify each vertebrate group from its characteristics and add the correct headings to each column. Add an example animal to each column.

Group					
Characteristics	Feathers Warm blooded Can fly	Fur Warm blooded Gives birth to live young	Gills Cold blooded Scales	Dry skin Cold blooded Lay eggs with soft shells	Moist skin Cold blooded Lay eggs in jelly
Example					

Activity 6: Invertebrate groups

Draw a line to match each invertebrate to the invertebrate group it belongs to.

Molluscs – soft unsegmented body, live in damp places, most have a shell

Arthropods – has an exoskeleton and a segmented body

Echinodermata – live in the sea and are often symmetrical

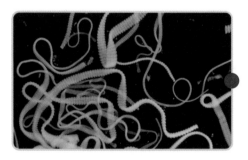

Flatworms – have a simple flattened body which does not have blood vessels

Annelids – segmented worms

Activity 7: Arthropods

Write how many legs each arthropod has.

Vertebrates and invertebrates can be classified into even smaller groups based on their characteristics.

For example, arthropods (an invertebrate group) can be divided into four smaller groups by looking at the number of legs different animals have.

Arthropod group	Example	Number of legs
Insects		
Arachnids		
Crustaceans		
Myriapods		

Key learning

In this lesson I have learned that: **Organisms** are **classified** into five main groups (called **kingdoms**), based on their characteristics. These are plants, animals, **fungi**, and the microorganisms, **protista** and **monera**. Plants are classified into flowering and non-flowering. Animals are classified into **vertebrates** and **invertebrates**. Vertebrates can be classified into five groups: reptiles, amphibians, mammals, fish and birds. Invertebrates can be classified into molluscs, arthropods, flatworm, annelids, echinodermata. Arthropods can be classified into four groups depending on the number of legs they have. These are – insects, arachnids, crustaceans and myriapods.

Homework

Find out more about a living thing you had not heard of before this lesson. Find out what classification group it belongs. Draw and label your living thing. Explain what features it shares with the other living things in the same group.

Key vocabulary

cone	fern	moss	spore
conifer	flowering plant	reproduction	

Activity 1: Classifying plants

Look at the pictures and features of each of the groups of plants below.

Flowering plant
Key features: flowers for reproduction; stems, roots and leaves.

dandelion

Ferns
Key features: No flowers; produce spores for reproduction; leaves, stems and roots.

ostrich fern

Conifers
Key features: usually evergreen and can be a tree or a shrub; narrow pointed leaves and cones where seeds are grown for reproduction.

Scots pine

Mosses
Key features: No flowers; produce spores for reproduction; stems and leaves; no roots.

common tamarisk

Write the group name for each plant in the chart below.

List the features of the plant that helped you to choose the correct group.

Add other examples using your own research.

Plant	Features	Examples
Group:  _____ _____	_____ _____ _____ _____ _____	_____ _____ _____ _____ _____
Group:  _____ _____	_____ _____ _____ _____ _____	_____ _____ _____ _____ _____
Group:  _____ _____	_____ _____ _____ _____	_____ _____ _____ _____
Group:  _____ _____	_____ _____ _____ _____	_____ _____ _____ _____

Activity 2: Plant groups

Decide if each statement is true or false. Circle the correct answer.

Flowering plants use flowers for reproduction.	True	False
Conifers produce spores for reproduction.	True	False
Ferns, mosses and conifers are plants that do not have flowers.	True	False
Mosses do not have roots.	True	False
Ferns produce cones.	True	False

Key learning

In this lesson I have learned that: Plants are classified into four main groups based on similar characteristics: **Flowering plants** have roots, leaves and stems. They have flowers for **reproduction** to make seeds and grow new plants. **Ferns** have roots, stems and leaves but they do not have flowers. They reproduce by producing **spores** (which are like seeds). **Conifers** have roots, stems and narrow pointed leaves (called needles). They do not have flowers, but reproduce by growing seeds inside **cones**. **Mosses** have stems and leaves but no roots or flowers. They reproduce by producing spores.

Homework

Look for conifers, ferns and mosses on your journey to and from school. Decide which type of plant you have found. Write down what you found and where you found it.

Key vocabulary

classification   invertebrates   organism   vertebrates

Activity 1: Classifying animals

Explain what is meant by an observable characteristic.

_____

_____

Carry out research to complete the information.

Mammals are vertebrates / invertebrates.
(Circle the correct answer.)

Write one example of a mammal:

_____

mammal

Write two common characteristics
of mammals:

_____

_____

Birds are vertebrates / invertebrates.
(Circle the correct answer.)

Write one example of a bird:

_____

bird

Write two common characteristics
of birds:

_____

_____

Reptiles are vertebrates / invertebrates.
(Circle the correct answer.)

Write one example of a reptile:

_____

reptile

Write two common characteristics
of reptiles:

_____

_____

Amphibians are vertebrates /
invertebrates.
(Circle the correct answer.)

Write one example of an amphibian:

_____

amphibian

Write two common characteristic
of amphibians:

_____

_____

Fish are vertebrates / invertebrates.
(Circle the correct answer.)

Write one example of a fish:

_____

fish

Write two common characteristics
of fish:

_____

_____

Insects are vertebrates / invertebrates.
(Circle the correct answer.)

Write one example of an insect:

_____

insect

Write two common characteristics
of insects:

_____

_____

Arachnids are vertebrates / invertebrates.
(Circle the correct answer.)

Write one example of an arachnid:

_____

arachnid

Write two common characteristics
of arachnids:

_____

_____

Crustaceans are vertebrates / invertebrates.
(Circle the correct answer.)

Write one example of a crustacean:

_____

crustacean

Write two common characteristics
of crustaceans:

_____

_____

Myriapods are vertebrates / invertebrates.
(Circle the correct answer.)

Write one example of a myriapod:

_____

myriapod

Write two common characteristics
of myriapods:

_____

_____

Molluscs are vertebrates / invertebrates.
(Circle the correct answer.)

Write one example of a mollusc:

_____

mollusc

Write two common characteristics
of molluscs:

_____

_____

Annelids are vertebrates / invertebrates.
(Circle the correct answer.)

Write one example of an annelid:

_____

annelid

Write two common characteristics
of annelids:

_____

_____

Activity 2: What is a mammal?

The bottle nose dolphin is a mammal.

List the three characteristics of a mammal that a dolphin has.

_____

_____

_____

Name a characteristic of a mammal that a dolphin does not have.

_____

Key learning

In this lesson I have learned that: **Organisms** are **classified** into groups based on their characteristics. Animals can be classified as **vertebrates** or **invertebrates**. Vertebrates can be classified as birds, fish, mammals, amphibians and reptiles. Invertebrates can be classified as arthropods, molluscs, annelids, flatworms and echinodermata. Arthopods can be classified as insects, arachnids, crustaceans and myriapods. You can use common observable characteristics to group animals.

Homework

Choose a whale, a platypus or a bat. Find out which vertebrate group your organism belongs to, which common characteristics it has and which characteristic it is missing.

Key vocabulary

fungi   monera   mould   organism   protista

Activity 1: What are the best conditions for mould to grow on bread?

You are going to carry out an enquiry to investigate what the best conditions are for mould to grow on bread. Plan your enquiry by discussing the following questions with a partner.

Which variables need to stay the same?

How will you measure mould growth?

What variables need to change?

How often will you take measurements?

Explain what 'best' conditions are.

_____

_____

Predict the best conditions for mould to grow in.

_____

_____

Explain how you are going to carry out your enquiry.

_____

_____

_____

_____

_____

List the equipment you are going to use.

_____

_____

Write the results of your enquiry.

_____

_____

_____

_____

Write your conclusion. Explain what conditions were best for mould to grow and how you know this.

_____

_____

Activity 2: Comparing plants and fungi

Some plants and fungi look similar. Complete the table to show how fungi and plants are different. The first example has been done for you.

Characteristic	Plants	Fungi
Have roots	✓	✗
Make their own food		
Reproduce using seeds		
Reproduce using spores		

Key learning

In this lesson I have learned that: Organisms are **classified** into five kingdoms: plants, animals, **fungi**, **protista** and **monera**. Protista and monera are groups of microorganisms. They are so small that they can only be seen with a microscope. They are very simple **organisms** and have only one main part. Fungi contain a wide range of organisms; some fungi look a bit like plants. Others, like **mould**, are microscopic.

Homework

Many people think all microorganisms are harmful and make you ill. But some are actually really helpful. Find out about useful bacteria.

Key vocabulary

branching key   organism

Activity 1: Using a branching key

Look at this branching key.

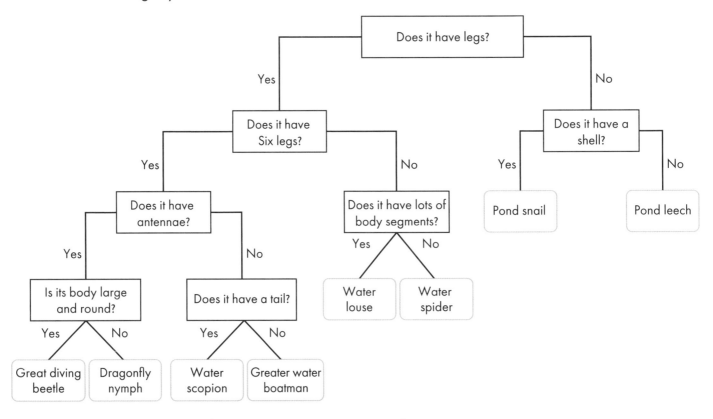

Use the branching key to identify organism A, organism B and organism C.

A

B

C

_____   _____   _____

Create a branching key for the following animals:

brown centipede

giant African millipede

great diving beetle

red wood ant

greater water boatman

The key has been started for you.

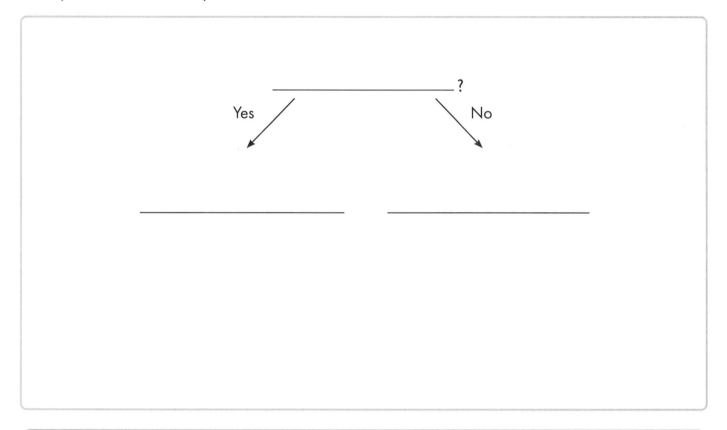

_____ ?

Yes /   No

Key learning

In this lesson I have learned that: Unknown **organisms** can be identified using a **branching key**. By asking a series of yes/no questions, based on common observable characteristics, we can start to identify organisms and name them.

Homework

Make a branching key to identify some different items, such as a set of books or some toys from home, or even a football team. Ask someone to try using your key to see if it works.

Key vocabulary

organism   species

Activity 1: Organism hunt

Observe six different organisms. Look for organisms in your local area – in a pond, in the garden, in the playground – or look at the organisms brought into school by your teacher.

Write field notes, with a sketch and a list of observable characteristics, for each organism.

Organism 1 _____

Sketch	Notes

Organism 2 _____

Sketch	Notes

Organism 3 _____

Sketch	Notes

Organism 4 _____

Sketch	Notes

Organism 5 _____

Sketch	Notes

Key learning

In this lesson I have learned that: If you look closely, you will find lots of difference **species** of organisms living in your local area. You can use a **branching key** to identify and name the species.

Homework

Look for organisms on your journey to and from school. Look out for the organisms you identified in this lesson.

Key vocabulary

organism   species

Activity 1: Design a branching key

Design a branching key to identify some of the organisms you found in your local area or your teacher brought into school.

The key has been started for you.

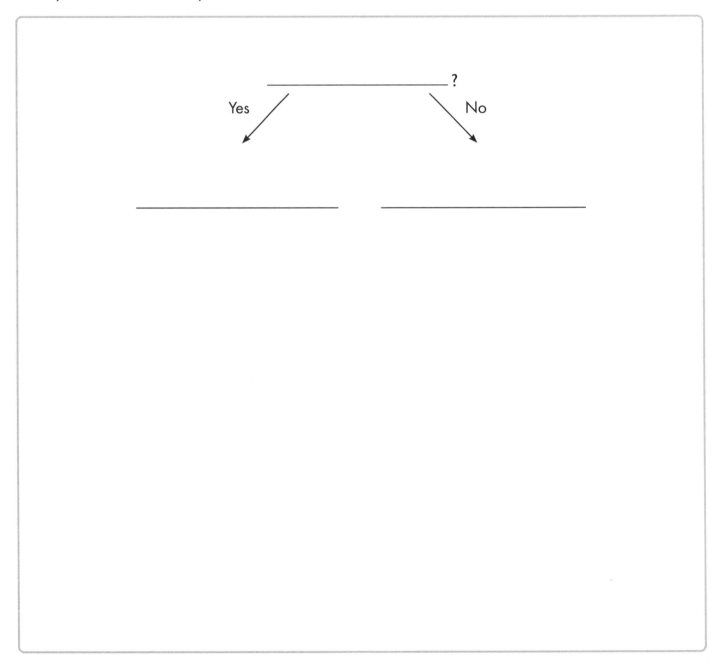

Activity 2: Identifying organisms

Explain how you ensured that each organism was put in the correct place in your branching key.

_____

_____

List five key facts that you have learned in this module.

1 _____

_____

2 _____

_____

3 _____

_____

4 _____

_____

5 _____

_____

Key learning

In this lesson I have learned that: A **branching key** can identify the name of an unknown **organism**.

Homework

Branching keys are one way of finding out the name of an unknown organism. Search for three other ways of identifying unknown species.

Evolution and inheritance

Lesson 1 · How are living things different?

Key vocabulary

classify	organism	reproduction	variation
offspring	reproduce	species	

Activity 1: The same or different?

Look at the two organisms (living things) below. List the ways in which they are different and similar in the Venn diagram. We use the word variation to talk about the difference between organisms.

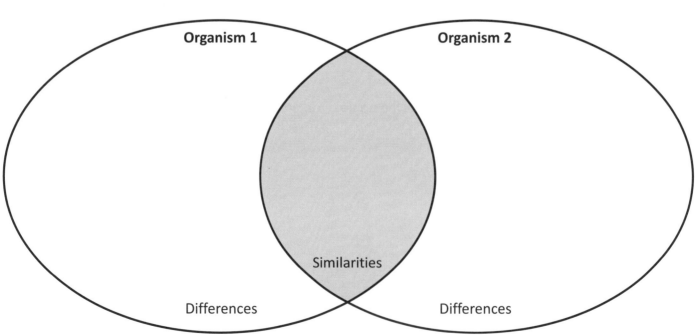

Organism 1   Organism 2

Similarities

Differences   Differences

Activity 2: Species

A group of organisms that are similar to each other, can reproduce and have offspring that can then have their own offspring is called a species. Variation happens within a species as well as between different species.

Look at these different pairs of organisms. Write whether the animals in each pair are from the same species or not. Explain how you know.

bear

tortoise

Circle the correct answer, then complete the sentence.

These animals are/are not from the same species.

I know this because _____

_____

labrador

poodle

Circle the correct answer, then complete the sentence.

These animals are/are not from the same species.

I know this because _____

_____

horse

zebra

Circle the correct answer, then complete the sentence.

These animals are/are not from the same species.

I know this because _____

_____

Activity 3: How are living things different?

You will need

- a tape measure
- a calculator

Humans are all the same species. Vitruvius, a Roman architect and engineer, believed that a human's height was the same as their arm span. You are going to find out if he was right! Work with a group to measure each other's height and arm span.

Name	Height	Arm span

Compare your results with other groups. Look for a pattern in your results. Decide if you have enough data to prove whether Vitruvius was right. Write about your findings.

_____

_____

_____

Key learning

In this lesson I have learned that: An **organism** is a living thing. We can **classify** living things into groups by looking at their similarities. A group of organisms that are very similar to each other and can **reproduce offspring** is called a **species**. The differences between species is known as **variation**. There are also differences between individuals within the same species, and this is also called variation.

Homework

Repeat the investigation at home by recording the height and arm span of friends and family.

Key vocabulary

adaptation   adapted   camouflage   habitat   migrate

Activity 1: Plant adaptations

What do plants need to survive? List three things.

1 _____ 2. _____ 3. _____

Any feature that helps a plant or animal to survive is called an adaptation. Plants and animals are adapted to survive in specific habitats.

Research these plants and their habitats. Complete the sentences.

Cacti

Cacti are adapted to live in:

_____

List three adaptations that cacti have:

_____

_____

_____

These adaptations help cacti to survive in the habitat because:

_____

_____

_____

Cushion plant

Cushion plants are usually found in cold, windy habitats, where there are few nutrients in the soil.

List three adaptations that cushion plants have:

_____

_____

_____

These adaptations help cushion plants to survive in the habitat because:

_____

_____

_____

Activity 2: How is an organism adapted to live in its habitat?

Choose one of the following animals, or a different animal of your own choice, to investigate. Use secondary sources of information to find out how your chosen animal is adapted to survive in its environment.

gentoo penguin

northern crested newt

fennec fox

Animal name: _____

What the habitat is like: _____

_____

What they eat: _____

How they get their food: _____

How they stop themselves being eaten: _____

_____

How they get water: _____

How they make sure they do not get too hot or too cold: _____

_____

Where they shelter: _____

Any other survival features or behaviours: _____

_____

Key learning

In this lesson I have learned that: Any feature that helps an organism to survive in its **habitat** is called an **adaptation**. Plants and animals are adapted to survive in specific habitats. Adaptations can be physical features, like **camouflaged** fur or skin. Adaptations can also be behaviours, like **migrating** to a new habitat at different times of the year.

Homework

Choose another animal or plant to research. Describe its adaptations and explain how they help it to survive in its habitat.

Key vocabulary

adaptation   habitat   species
adapted   predator
extinction / extinct   reproduction / reproduce

Activity 1: Different habitats

Gentoo penguins live around Antarctica. Northern crested newts live in forests around Europe.

gentoo penguin

northern crested newt

Does the gentoo penguin have any adaptations that would help it to survive in a forest? Explain your answer.

_____

_____

Predict what might happen to the gentoo penguin if it was moved to a forest habitat.

_____

_____

Does the northern crested newt have any adaptations that would help it to survive in Antarctica? Explain your answer.

_____

_____

Predict what might happen to the northern crested newt if it was moved to Antarctica.

_____

_____

Activity 2: Animal adaptations

Look at these five imaginary habitats.

Habitat A

Holey island – This habitat is surrounded by sea water and has many high mountains. Fast flowing rivers travel from the top of the mountains to the sea. The island is cold and does not support much plant life. Small mammals live on the island but spend the majority of their time in deep, complex tunnels.

Habitat B

Dangerous skies – This habitat is very flat; there are no hills or mountains. There are a number of larger lakes and each lake has short trees and shrubs growing around it. Small mammals feed off the trees and shrubs. The main predators in the area are very large, aggressive birds.

Habitat C

Fast moving food – This habitat is a jungle that is hot and humid day and night. There is a huge amount of plant life, but the majority of the edible leaves and berries are very high in the canopy. The jungle also supports large lizards that are not dangerous but can move extremely quickly.

Habitat D

Thin ice – This habitat is very cold and windy. There is hardly any plant life. The majority of the environment is made up of very thin ice. There are a number of large and small fish living underneath the ice.

Habitat E

Hot and bothered – This habitat is very hot and contains a number of active volcanoes that erupt unpredictably. The lava has formed small islands of rock. Each rock supports a small amount of plant life, together with small insects and mammals. If an animal fed off one rock for too long, the plants, insects and mammals would very quickly run out.

Choose one of the habitats and design an animal that could survive in that habitat. Give your animal the adaptations it needs to survive in the habitat. Use the space below to draw and label your animal.

I choose habitat _____

My animal is called _____

Explain how your animal adapted to its habitat. Think about what it eats, how it stays alive and how it protects itself from predators (such as by using camouflage, spikes, poison and so on), how it reproduces and where it shelters.

_____

_____

Key learning

In this lesson I have learned that: Animals are **adapted** to survive in a particular **habitat**. They find ways to get enough food and water, to avoid **predators**, and to **reproduce**. If the habitat changes, the animals' adaptations might not be helpful anymore. Some animals could die. If all animals of the same **species die**, that species will be **extinct**.

Homework

Research an animal or plant that you're interested in. Describe its adaptations and explain how it is adapted to survive in its habitat.

Lesson 4 · What can fossils tell us?

Key vocabulary

adaptation   evidence   evolution/evolve   extinction/extinct   fossil

Activity 1: Fossils

Fossils can give us information about organisms that have become extinct. Organisms can become extinct where their habitat changes. When a habitat changes, the organism's **adaptations** are no longer suited to helping it survive there.

Tyrannosaurus rex

Look at this fossil of a Tyrannosaurus rex skeleton. Decide what you can learn about the dinosaur from its skeleton. Tick 'true' or 'false' for each statement.

Tick (✓) the correct box to show what you can learn about Tyrannosaurus rex from its fossil.

	True	False		True	False
Height	☐	☐	How fast it could run	☐	☐
Length	☐	☐	What colour its skin was	☐	☐
Weight	☐	☐	What it sounded like	☐	☐
Number of teeth	☐	☐	What it ate	☐	☐

This is a fossil of Ichthyosaur (ick-thee-uh-saw). It lived 250 to 90 million years ago.

List the things you can tell about Ichthyosaur from its fossil.

_____

_____

_____

_____

This is a picture of how scientists believed Ichthyosaur looked. Compare it to your own ideas.

What kind of habitat do you think Ichthyosaur lived in? Write and explain your answer.

_____

_____

_____

_____

Activity 2: Archaeopteryx

This is the fossilised skeleton of Archaeopteryx (ar-key-op-ter-rix). An artist has drawn a more detailed image of the fossil.

Draw a picture of what you think Archaeopteryx looked like when it was alive. You can draw it in a different position. Annotate your drawing to explain some of its adaptations and what you think its habitat was like.

Activity 3: How might Eohippus have changed into a horse?

Not all fossils are of animals that became extinct. Fossils can also help us to understand how animals change into different animals over millions of years. This scientific theory of change is called evolution. Horses are believed to have evolved from Eohippus (ee-ow-hi-puhs).

Look at each animal and its skeleton.

Eohippus was about 30cm tall

 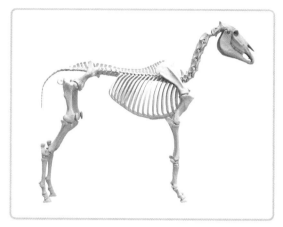

Modern horses are about 150cm tall

List the ways Eohippus changed when it evolved into a modern horse.

_____

_____

_____

_____

_____

_____

_____

Key learning

In this lesson I have learned that: **Fossils** are the remains of living things. They are **evidence** of the organisms that lived on Earth millions of years ago. Fossils usually come from hard parts of the body, like bones, teeth, claws and shells. Fossils are evidence of species that are **extinct**. They can also show how one species **evolved** into another.

Homework

Choose an extinct animal or plant to research. Explain how and why it became extinct.

Key vocabulary

evolution/evolve	natural selection	variation
identical	offspring	
inherited/inherit	reproduction/reproduce	

Activity 1: Are they identical?

These kittens have the same mother and father. Look carefully at the photo.

Are the kittens **identical**? Yes ☐   No ☐

Activity 2: What are the offspring like?

When two animals or plants from the same species reproduce, they create offspring. Look at the features the Labradoodle has inherited from its parents. Complete the sentences using the words in the box.

labrador

poodle

labradoodle

The Labrador, Poodle and Labradoodle are all from the same _____ but they

are different breeds. Labradors and Poodles can _____ . Their

_____ will _____ features from both _____ , but these

features will not be _____ .

species

inherit

parents

identical

reproduce

offspring

There is variation within the same species. This means that some individuals will be better adapted to survive in the habitat, should it change. The individuals with the survival adaptation are more likely to reproduce and create offspring that also have the adaptation to survive. Therefore, those offspring are more likely to survive in the changed habitat. This is known in science as natural selection.

Look at these images about natural selection.

Describe the variation within this species. Look at their bodies, legs and beaks to see if anything is different.

How has the habitat changed in this picture? Look at the sea, mountains and plants to find what is different.

_____

How will the variation in this species help them to survive in the changed habitat?

_____

Which individuals are most likely to reproduce?

_____

Which adaptation are their offspring likely to have?

_____

Put these statements in the correct order to explain the process of natural selection. Number the statements from 1 to 5.

☐ **The individuals with the survival adaptation are more likely to reproduce.**

☐ **Some individuals have adaptations which make them more likely to survive.**

☐ **Their offspring are more likely to have the survival adaptation.**

☐ **There is variation within the same species.**

☐ **There is a change in the habitat of the species.**

Activity 4: The bird beaks game

Play the bird beaks game together as a class. You have one minute to get 15 grains of rice or more into the cup using the different utensils. The utensils represent different bird beaks, the rice is the bird's food and the cup is the bird's stomach. Note down how much rice you were able to put in the cup with each utensil.

What was the best 'beak' (utensil) for 'eating' rice?

_____

Repeat the game using marbles instead of rice.

What was the best 'beak' (utensil) for 'eating' marbles?

_____

You will need

- large beakers (one per table)
- a large bag of uncooked rice
- cups (one per child)
- utensils: tweezers, tongs, knives and forks (enough for each child to have one utensil, plus extras, particularly of the tweezers and tongs)
- timers
- set of marbles
- set of scales

Use the table below to record your results from playing the game.

Beak (utensil)	Food (rice or marbles)	Amount collected

Key learning

In this lesson I have learned that: Animals of the same species have lots of similarities, but they also have some **variations**. If the habitat changes, some of these variations can mean those living things are more likely to survive and **reproduce**. Their **offspring** then **inherit** the variation. This process has the scientific name of **natural selection**.

Key vocabulary

evolution/evolve   natural selection   offspring   reproduction/reproduce

Activity 1: Survival of the fittest

arctic fox

Look at the pictures and answer the questions.

Arctic fox

What features might help some Arctic foxes to survive if there was less ice?

_____

_____

_____

_____

Which individuals would be the fittest now? Which would survive?

_____

_____

_____

Barn swallow

What features might help some swallows to survive if there were fewer flies to eat?

_____

_____

_____

barn swallow

Which individuals would be the fittest now? Which would survive?

_____

_____

_____

_____

Activity 2: The giraffe and the okapi

giraffe

okapi

Scientists think giraffes evolved from an animal like the okapi, because there wasn't enough food at ground level.

Use natural selection to explain how these scientists believe that the giraffe came to have its long neck.

_____

_____

_____

Write numbers 1-5 to order the steps of natural selection.

Step [ ] : The individuals with the survival adaptation are more likely to **reproduce**.

Step [ ] : There is a change in the habitat of the species.

Step [ ] : There is variation within the same species.

Step [ ] : Their **offspring** are more likely to have the survival adaptation.

Step [ ] : Some individuals have adaptations which make them more likely to survive.

Activity 3: Darwin and Wallace

Charles Darwin and Alfred Wallace were two scientists that came up with the theory of evolution. Research either Charles Darwin or Alfred Wallace. Use the prompts to help you.
Record your research in the box below.

You will need

- access to texts and web-based information about Charles Darwin and Alfred Wallace

Charles Darwin

- What observations did Darwin make about finches when he was on the Galapagos Islands?
- What observations did he make about tortoises when he was on the Galapagos Islands?
- How did these observations help him to come up with the idea of natural selection?

Alfred Wallace

- What observations did Wallace make when he was in the Amazon?
- What observations did he make when he was in the Malay Archipelago?
- How did these observations help him to come up with the idea of natural selection?

Key learning

In this lesson I have learned that: Charles Darwin and Alfred Wallace were both scientists. They each came up with the theory of **evolution** around the same time. Darwin worked in the Galapagos Islands, and Wallace worked in the Amazon and the Malay Archipelago. Wallace wrote to Darwin and they realised they had very similar ideas about **natural selection**, or the 'survival of the fittest'.

Homework

Research whichever of Darwin or Wallace you didn't choose in the lesson. You might also research the work of Emma Dunne or Telma Laurentino.

Module 3

What light does

Lesson 1 — How does light travel?

Key vocabulary

light ray   light source   opaque   reflect   shadow

Activity 1: What is a light source?

List some light sources that you saw on your way to school this morning.

_____

Is the classroom window a light source? Tick (✓) the correct answer: Yes ☐   No ☐

Explain your answer.

_____

_____

Activity 2: How does light travel?

You will need

- three pieces of card
- a light source
- sticky tack
- a hole punch
- a ruler
- uncooked spaghetti

Shine your light source on a wall or screen.

Hold up a piece of card between the wall and the light source and observe what happens.

Complete the sentence to explain what you observed, using the words in the box to help you.

| shadow |
| blocks |
| opaque |

When we hold a piece of card between the wall and the light source, _____

_____

_____

Punch a hole in the same place in three pieces of card.

Shine the light so that it passes through all three holes and reaches the wall.

Can you thread a piece of spaghetti through the three pieces of card at the same time?

Tick (✓) the correct answer: Yes ☐ No ☐

Explain what this tells you about how light travels.

_____

_____

_____

wall

cards

sticky tack

table top

torch (light source)

Activity 3: Hose test

Shine a torch down a straight, vertical length of hosepipe held above a desk. Use a piece of spaghetti to represent light rays and drop it down the hosepipe.

Complete each sentence.

I predict that if I shine light down a bent tube _____

_____

If light can travel along a curved or angled path, when I shine light down a bent tube _____

_____

Bend the hosepipe and try to shine the light onto the desk.

Complete the sentence.

Light travels _____

Draw a diagram of your hosepipe test.

straight pipe   **bent pipe**

Write some sentences to explain what the hosepipe test proves about how light travels.

_____

_____

_____

_____

Activity 4: Light rays

Draw lines on the diagram to show how light rays travel from a light source into our eyes so that we can see.

Key learning

In this lesson I have learned that: **Light rays** travel from a **light source**. The light enters our eyes and allows us to see. It is important not to look directly at some very bright light sources, like the Sun. Light always travels in straight lines. If an **opaque** object blocks the light, a **shadow** is created.

Homework

Think of any evidence from your daily life that proves light travels in straight lines. Talk about your ideas with family and friends.

Key vocabulary

dark	light source	shadow	variable
light	opaque	translucent	

Activity 1: Shadows

Use what you already know about shadows to label and add shading to the diagram below. Use the words in the box to help you – you don't need to use them all.

block light	light ray
light source	object
shadow	triangle
torch	

Write sentences to explain:

- how light can create a shadow
- what we can change about a shadow
- why we cannot change the shape of a shadow.

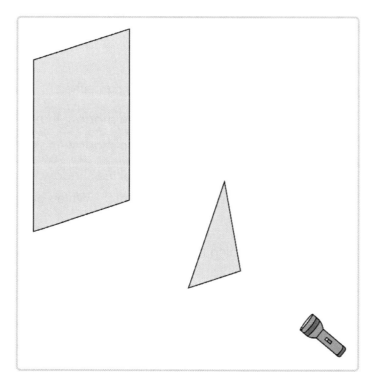

_____

_____

_____

_____

Complete the sentence.

If the object making the shadow was translucent, the shadow would be _____

because _____

_____

Activity 2: Making predictions about shadows

Use the sticky tack to hold the screen and shadow-maker in place on the table.

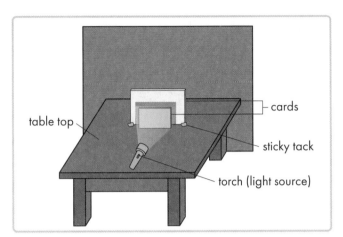

table top
cards
sticky tack
torch (light source)

You will need
- a torch
- a screen
- a shadow-maker (something that will make a clear shadow)
- sticky tack
- uncooked spaghetti

Choose one variable to change. You can either:

- change the distance between the shadow-maker and the screen
- change the distance between the shadow-maker and the torch.

Predict what will happen to the size of the shadow. You can use the spaghetti to help you see where the light rays will go. Do not turn on the torch! Write your prediction below. You will be doing the enquiry in the next lesson.

The variable I am going to change is _____

I predict that _____

_____

Key learning

In this lesson I have learned that: **Light** comes from a **light source**. If the light is blocked by an **opaque** object, it will cast a **shadow**. **Translucent** objects are objects that are almost see-through and they cast pale shadows as they allow some of the light to pass through them. We can experiment with shadows by looking at different **variables**.

Homework

Find out about Ibn al-Haytham and the experiments that he did to test his ideas. Create a factfile to bring into class.

Lesson 3 What might affect the size of a shadow?

Key vocabulary

light | light ray | light source | shadow

Activity 1: Planning an enquiry

You are going to plan an enquiry to test the prediction you made in the last lesson. Complete this table to make sure you plan a fair test.

We are investigating...Tick (✓) one • What happens when I change the distance between the shadow-maker and the screen ☐ • What happens when I change the distance between the shadow-maker and the torch. ☐				
We could change the following things:				
We could measure and observe the following things:				
We will change (independent variable):				
We will measure/observe (dependent variable):				
Our question is:				
We will keep these things the same (controlled variables):				

I predict that ____

____

Activity 2: Conducting a fair test

Conduct your test and record your measurements in this table.

You will need

- a torch
- sticky tack
- a screen
- a ruler or tape measure
- a shadow-maker

What I am changing (independent variable): (units: _____)	What I have observed/measured (dependent variable): (units: _____)			
	Test 1	Test 2	Test 3	Test 4

Explain whether your enquiry was a fair test or not. _____

_____

Explain why your readings were or were not what you expected. _____

_____

Explain what you found out about shadows. _____

Key learning

In this lesson I have learned that: **Light** comes from a **light source**. When **light rays** are blocked by an opaque object, a **shadow** is cast. Light rays always travel in a straight line. Changing a variable, such as the distance between the torch and the object will affect the size of the shadow.

Key vocabulary

data   opaque   pattern   prediction   shadow

Activity 1: Pattern in the data

Another class has conducted a fair test enquiry. They looked at how the height of the object affected the height of the shadow.

Use the data in the table to plot the points on the graph. Then join the dots together with a line.

Heigh of object (cm)	Height of shadow (cm)
1	2
2	4
3	6
4	8
5	10

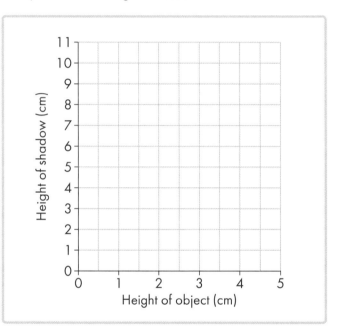

Which of these statements about the graph is correct? Tick (✓) the correct answer.

1. When the height of the object (independent variable) was increased, the height of the shadow (dependent variable) increased. ☐

2. When the height of the object (independent variable) was increased, the height of the shadow (dependent variable) decreased. ☐

Activity 2: Plotting your results

Use the data from the fair test enquiry you carried out in the last lesson to plot a line graph. Your line graph may show a straight or a curved line.

My enquiry question is: _____

Describe the shape of the graph. _____

Circle the answer then complete the sentence.

The graph matches/does not match the prediction I made in Lesson 2.

This tells me _____

_____

_____

Key learning

In this lesson I have learned that: Working scientifically involves making **predictions**, collecting **data** and then looking at the data to spot any **patterns**. We know that a **shadow** will be created when light rays are blocked by an **opaque** object because light rays travel in straight lines. The size of the shadow depends on a variety of factors. Changing a variable, such as the distance between the torch and the object will affect the size of the shadow.

Homework

Think about the variable that you did not test. Predict what you would find out if you tested this variable.

Key vocabulary

light	light source	reflection
light ray	reflect	reflective

Activity 1: Reflecting light

Set your equipment up as shown in the picture below. Shine the torch and watch how the light reflects off the mirror. Draw the path of the light on the diagram

You will need
- a torch
- two cards with slits in them
- a mirror
- sticky tack

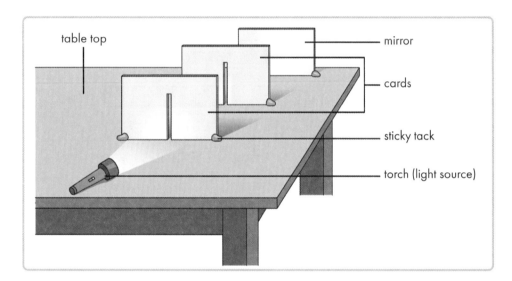

Now change the angle of the mirror as shown in the diagram below. Shine the torch and watch how the light reflects off the mirror. Draw the path of the light on the diagram.

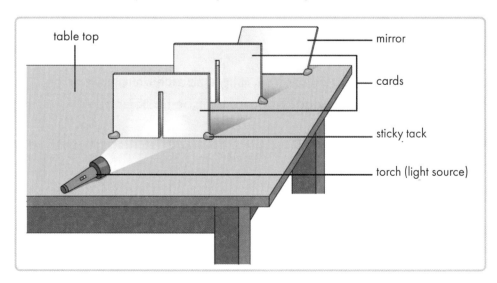

Activity 2: Mirror maze

Set up a light source and a screen with an eye drawn on the same side of a table, and at least 20cm apart.

Use mirrors to direct the light from the torch to the screen.

Use uncooked spaghetti to help you to work out where the light needs to go.

Where you have placed the mirrors, use spaghetti again to predict how the light will move.

Test your solution with the torch.

When you have succeeded, draw the mirrors and the direction of a light ray on the diagram with a ruler and pencil.

You will need
- a torch
- two mirrors
- a screen
- uncooked spaghetti

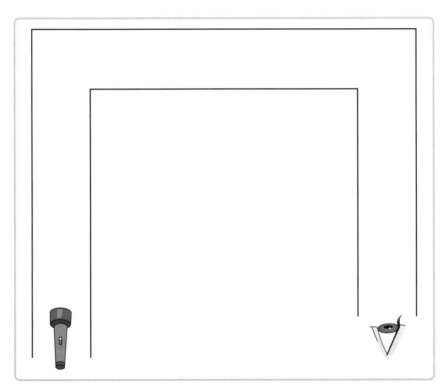

Key learning

In this lesson I have learned that: **Light** comes from a **light source** like a bulb or the Sun. **Light rays** travel in straight lines. Objects that are opaque absorb light. Some objects **reflect** light from their surface. We say they are **reflective**.

Homework

Find out what a sound echo is. Think about how a sound echo might link to what you have learned in this lesson.

Key vocabulary

light   light ray   light source   reflect   reflective

Activity 1: Exploring light

Look at some objects that are shiny and some objects that are not shiny. Think about what you have noticed, then tick (✓) 'true' or 'false' for each of these statements.

	TRUE	FALSE
All objects reflect light.		
All objects are reflective.		
Shiny objects are light sources.		
Dull objects reflect no light.		
Dull objects are poor reflectors of light.		
Light sources emit many light rays at once.		

Activity 2: Light models

Use your equipment to make a model that explains how we see an object.

Draw an eye on the mini whiteboard then arrange the other items to show how light rays travel to the eye.

When you have completed your model, draw and label a diagram in the space below.

You will need
- string
- arrow cards
- clips
- an object
- a torch
- a mini whiteboard

Key learning

In this lesson I have learned that: We see objects when a **light source** that falls on them is reflected into our eyes. All objects **reflect** some **light** or we would not be able to see them. Shiny objects like a mirror reflect a lot of light and can be seen in very dim light. Dull objects like a soft toy are poor reflectors of light. This is why it is hard to see them in very dim light.

Homework

Use a mirror to look at an object behind you or the back of your head. Draw a diagram to explain how you can see the object reflected in the mirror. Bring your drawing into school for discussion.

Human circulation

Lesson 1   What is blood made of?

Key vocabulary

blood vessels   oxygen   red blood cells
carbon dioxide   plasma   white blood cells
nutrients   platelets

Activity 1: What is blood made of?

As well as nutrients and water, blood also carries oxygen around the body. Oxygen is one of the gases in the air that we breathe in and that we need to live. Blood is contained in blood vessels, which are tubes that carry the blood to all the parts of our bodies.

Blood is made up of four different parts, as shown in this diagram.

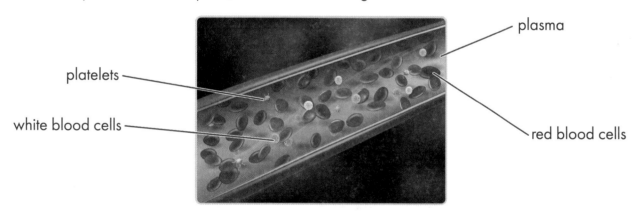

platelets

white blood cells

plasma

red blood cells

Use the information you have found out and the words in the box to complete the sentences below.

Blood is made up of _____ different parts. The _____

transports nutrients and waste products. Oxygen is transported by

_____ , which also carry away carbon dioxide.

We are protected from infections by _____ , and _____

stop wounds from bleeding by forming blood clots.

| plasma |
| red blood cells |
| platelets |
| white blood cells |
| four |

Activity 2: Blood fact files

Create a fact file for each part of the blood. Use secondary sources of information to help you.

Part of the blood: **red blood cells**

Job: _____

Makes up _____ per cent of blood.

Further facts:

_____

_____

_____

Part of the blood: **white blood cells**

Job: _____

Makes up _____ per cent of blood.

Further facts:

_____

_____

_____

Part of the blood: **platelets**

Job: _____

Makes up _____ per cent of blood.

Further facts:

_____

_____

_____

Part of the blood: **plasma**

Job: _____

Makes up _____ per cent of blood.

Further facts:

_____

_____

_____

Key learning

In this lesson I have learned that: Blood carries nutrients and water all around our body. Blood travels around our bodies in **blood vessels**. As well as **nutrients** and water, blood carries **oxygen** around the body. We need oxygen to live. Blood is made up of four different parts, **red blood cells**, **white blood cells**, **platelets** and **plasma**. Each part of blood has a different function. Red blood cells transport oxygen around the body and carry **carbon dioxide** away. White blood cells protect us from infection, platelets form blood clots to stop bleeding, and plasma transports nutrients and waste products.

Homework

Find out about blood donation and how donated blood helps save lives. If you know anyone who donates blood, ask them what happens and why they do it. Share what you have discovered with your classmates.

Key vocabulary

blood vessels
circulate/circulatory
deoxygenated blood

heart
lungs
nutrient

oxygen
oxygenated blood
system

Activity 1: What is a system?

Below are three body systems that you have already learnt about. Write what you remember about each system below the picture and label the pictures with the names of parts.

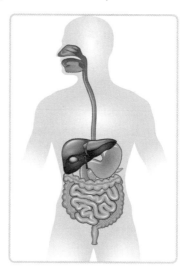

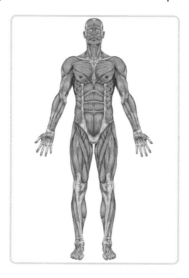

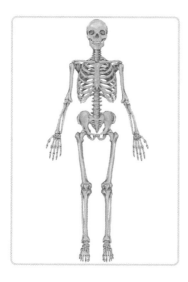

_____   _____   _____

_____   _____   _____

_____   _____   _____

_____   _____   _____

Work with a partner to agree a sentence that describes what a system is. Write it below.

_____

_____

_____

Activity 2: The circulatory system

Use the frame below to draw a simple diagram of the circulatory system.

- Draw the heart, the **lungs** and the body in the boxes.
- Add arrows to the lines to show the path of the blood.
- Label the different parts of the circulatory system.
- Add notes to explain what is happening at each point in the diagram.

Use the pictures here and your class roleplay of the circulatory system to help you.

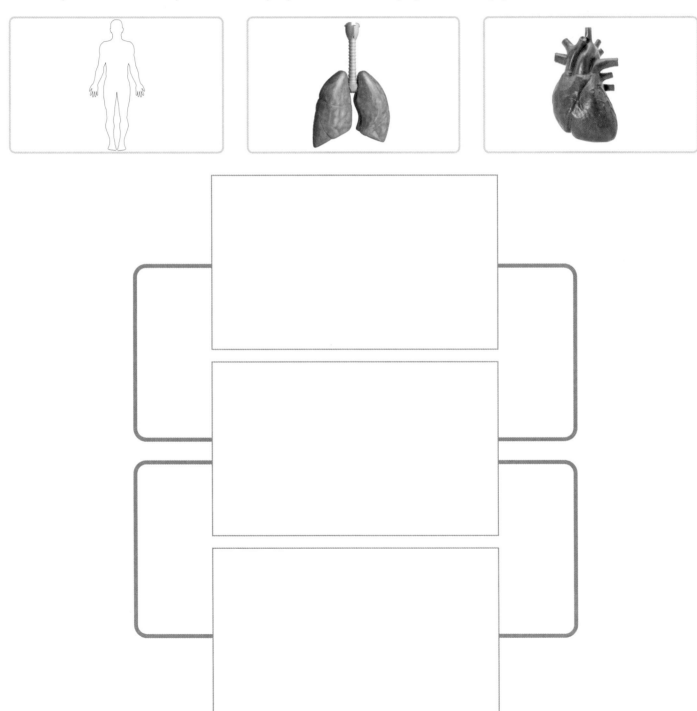

Activity 3: The heart

Look at the diagram of the heart below, then complete the sentences to explain how the heart works. Use the words in the box to help.

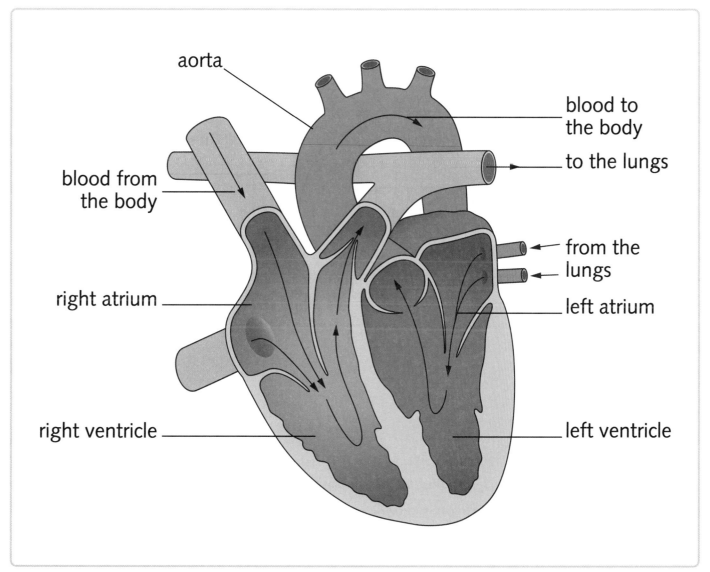

aorta

blood to the body

to the lungs

blood from the body

from the lungs

right atrium

left atrium

right ventricle

left ventricle

| oxygenated | deoxygenated | lungs | body | four |

The red parts of this diagram represent the _____ blood, which carries lots of oxygen.

The blue parts of this diagram represent the _____ , where the oxygen has been used up.

The **deoxygenated blood** is pumped to the _____ and the **oxygenated blood** is pumped

to _____ .

Use the words in the box to label this diagram of the heart.

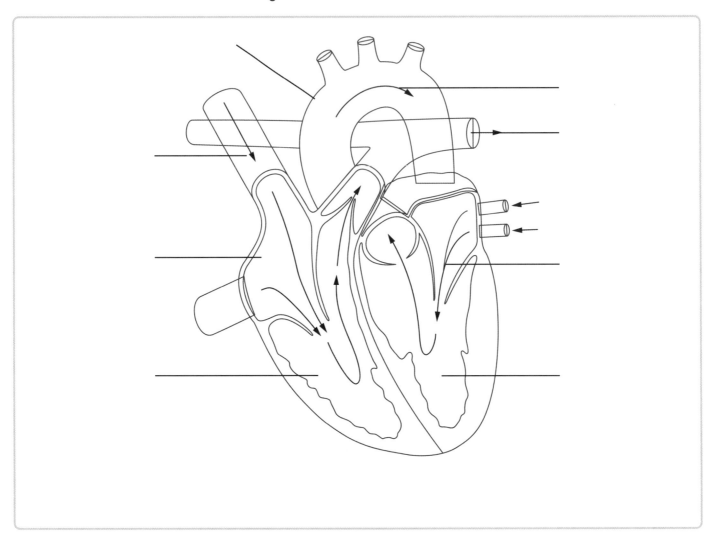

| to the lungs | to the rest of the body | left side of the heart |
| right side of the heart | oxygenated blood | deoxygenated blood |

Key learning

In this lesson I have learned that: Different parts of our body work together in different **systems**. We have a digestive system, a muscular system and a skeletal system. The **circulatory** system moves blood around the body to deliver **nutrients**, water and **oxygen**. The circulatory system is made up of the **heart**, **blood vessels** and blood.

Homework

Tell someone at home about what you have learned. Can you write three questions about the circulatory system to bring back into school and ask your classmates?

Key vocabulary

aorta	blood vessels	lungs	valve
atrium	chamber	oxygen	ventricle
blood	circulation	pulmonary artery	

Activity 1: The heart and the blood

Read the text below. Follow the path of blood around the heart on the diagram with your finger as you read.

As blood moves around the body, the oxygen is used up, so it returns to the lungs to pick up more. The heart is a muscle that moves the blood around the body. The deoxygenated blood enters the right atrium and goes into the right ventricle. When the heart pumps the deoxygenated blood leaves the heart through the pulmonary artery and goes to the lungs. Oxygenated blood from the lungs enters the left atrium and then the left ventricle. When the heart pumps, the oxygenated blood leaves the heart through the aorta on its way to the rest of the body. The valves in the heart stop the blood from flowing backwards.

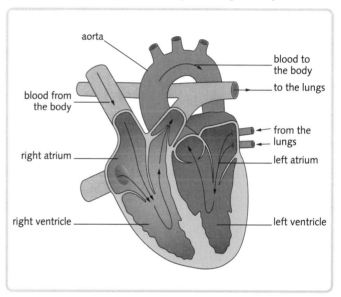

Activity 2: Making a model of the heart

Use the picture of the heart in activity 1 to help you make a 3D model of a human heart. Add labels to your model with cocktail sticks.

Draw your model below and include the labels.

Complete the checklist:

Have you included all the main parts? ☐

Have you made each part the right size and shape? ☐

Have you used different coloured clay to show the difference in the blood? ☐

Have you clearly labelled each part? ☐

Is the heart's function clear? ☐

You will need

- modelling clay in two colours
- a baseboard
- cocktail sticks
- labels

Activity 3: How does the heart pump blood around the body?

Draw lines to match each part of the heart to the explanation of what it is and does.

Aorta	The muscular organ that pumps your blood around your body.
Artery	Valves within the heart that open and close automatically to control blood flow into, through, and out of the heart.
Atrium	A blood vessel that carries blood away from the heart to the rest of the body.
Blood	One of the two upper chambers of the heart that collects blood as it enters the heart and before it is pumped to the ventricles.
Blood vessel	A fluid found in humans and other animals that provides nutrients and oxygen to all parts of the body. It carries away waste, and helps fight disease.
Chamber	Tubes that carry blood around the body.
Circulation	The largest artery in the body, which delivers blood from the heart to the rest of the body.
Heart	One of four sections of the heart, like rooms in the heart.
Heart valves	The movement of blood through the vessels.
Ventricle	One of the two lower chambers of the heart. The right ventricle sends blood to the lungs, and the left ventricle sends blood carrying oxygen to the rest of the body.

Key learning

In this lesson I have learned that: **Blood** must be pumped from the heart to the **lungs** to collect **oxygen**. Then it goes back to the heart to be pumped around the body. The deoxygenated blood enters the right **atrium** and goes into the right **ventricle**. When the heart pumps the deoxygenated blood leaves the heart through the **pulmonary artery** and goes to the lungs. Oxygenated blood from the lungs enters the left atrium and then the left ventricle. When the heart pumps, the oxygenated blood leaves the heart through the **aorta** on its way to the rest of the body. The **valves** in the heart stop the blood from flowing backwards.

Homework

Find out how you can look after your heart. Write a list of the three best things you can do to keep your heart healthy.

Lesson 4   What are blood vessels and valves and what do they do?

Key vocabulary

aorta   blood vessels   valve

arteries   capillaries   veins

Activity 1: Blood flow

Look at the diagram. The close-up images show one of the valves inside the heart. One diagram shows the valve open; the other shows it closed.

Label each valve diagram with the word 'open' or 'closed'.

Explain what would happen to the blood if the heart had no valves.

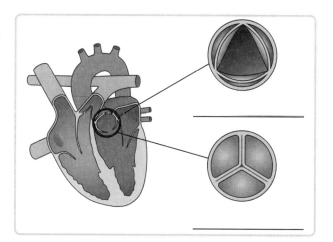

_____

_____

Activity 2: Blood vessels and valves

Use what you have learnt so far and secondary sources to find out more about arteries and veins.
Use the information to answer the questions below.

You will need

- books and online resources about blood vessels and valves

What is an artery?_____

What is a vein? _____

What does an artery carry? _____

Are there any exceptions? _____

What does a vein usually carry? _____

Are there any exceptions? _____

How is the wall of an artery different to the wall of a vein? _____

What do valves do? _____

How long would our circulatory system be if we pulled it out in one line? _____

What is the largest artery in our body? _____

Activity 3: Blood vessels and valves fact file

Use your research notes and answers from the last activity to complete these fact files.

Arteries

_____

_____

_____

outer layer — smooth muscle — elastic layer — inner layer

Veins

_____

_____

_____

outer layer — smooth muscle — inner layer — valve

Valves

_____

_____

_____

open

closed

Fun facts

_____

_____

_____

Key learning

In this lesson I have learned that: Blood travels around the body through different kinds of **blood vessels**. We have **arteries** that take blood away from the heart, and **veins** that take blood to the heart. The smallest blood vessels in our circulatory system are **capillaries**. Veins and arteries have **valves**, but capillaries do not. Valves stop blood from flowing backwards.

Homework

Share your fact file with an adult home. Find out what information was new to them. Ask them to tell you what they liked about your fact file.

Key vocabulary

blood	digestive system	nutrients	oxygen	water
blood vessels	large intestine	organ	small intestine	

Activity 1: What happens to water?

Look at this diagram and complete the sentences.

This diagram shows the _____ system.

Water enters the body through _____

_____

Draw on the diagram the path that water takes.

The water enters the blood _____

_____

What does blood carry around the body to keep us alive?
Circle the correct answers.

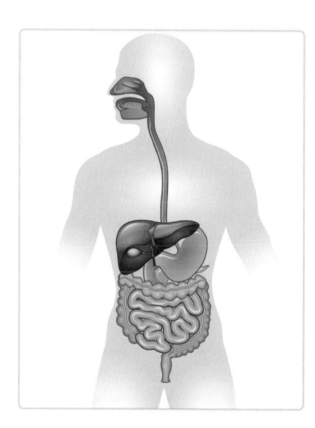

oxygen	large intestine	small
nutrients	intestine	heart	water

Activity 2: Wonderful water

Answer the following questions about water.

Why do we need water?

_____

What happens if we don't get enough water?

_____

Is all water the same?

_____

What happens if we get too much water?

_____

Discuss your ideas as a class and improve your answers above.

Activity 3: What did William Harvey find out about the circulatory system?

Read about the scientist William Harvey below and answer the questions.

William Harvey lived in the late 1500s and early 1600s. In those days, people still followed the ideas of Galen, who wrote about the human body in the second century. Galen was an ancient Greek. Galen thought that blood in the veins was made by the liver and contained nutrients. He thought that it flowed to the **organs** in the body, which used up that blood. He also believed that blood in the arteries was made by the heart and contained 'life spirit', which flowed to the organs in the body and used up that blood.

William Harvey observed the circulatory system in animals such as snakes and frogs. He could see that the blood circulated around the body, pumped by the heart. William Harvey suspected that quite a lot of the current ideas about blood were incorrect and, through his experiments, discovered that the amount of blood in the body is fixed, and that it circulates around the body, passing through the lungs and other organs. He also discovered valves and their function to stop the blood from flowing backwards.

William Harvey

Galen

What did William Harvey discover about blood?

_____

What did William Harvey discover about how blood travels around the body?

_____

What did people believe before William Harvey made his discoveries?

_____

Who was the other scientist whose theories were proven to be incorrect?

_____

Do animals such as snakes and frogs have circulatory systems?

_____

Activity 4: True or False?

Think about everything you have learned in this module. Tick (✓) 'true' or 'false' for each statement.

	TRUE	FALSE
The two chambers at the bottom of your heart are called ventricles.		
Blood vessels that carry blood towards your heart are called arteries.		
Your circulatory system helps transport water and nutrients to the rest of your body.		
We need to drink about six to eight glasses of water a day to maintain healthy hydration levels.		
The red blood cells in our blood fight infection.		
The plasma in our blood makes it red.		
Our blood is sometimes blue.		
Without platelets, our blood wouldn't clot when we cut ourselves.		
If we stand on our head no blood will get to our feet.		
The heart pumps blood around the body in a figure-of-eight system.		
The circulatory system is the only system in our bodies.		
Humans can survive for up to ten days without water.		

Key learning

In this lesson I have learned that: Our bodies need water for a variety of life functions. **Water** enters the body through the **digestive system** and is carried in the **blood**, along with **nutrients** from food and oxygen from the air we breathe. William Harvey was a scientist who discovered that the amount of blood in a body is fixed and that it is pumped around the body, passing through the lungs to collect **oxygen**. This is the circulatory system. He discovered this by conducting a variety of experiments. He also discovered valves and their function in the circulatory system. It is not only humans who have circulatory systems. Most vertebrates and some invertebrates have circulatory systems.

Homework

Studying blood can tell us a lot about how healthy we are or whether there are some problems inside our body. With an adult, use the internet to find out what information can be detected in a blood test.

Electricity: changing circuits

Lesson 1   **How do we light the lamp?**

Key vocabulary

battery	connection point	motor
buzzer	electrical component	switch
cell	electrical conductor	
circuit	lamp	

Activity 1: True or false?

Think about what you already know about electricity and making circuits. Tick (✓) 'true' or 'false' for each statement.

	TRUE	FALSE
A lamp-holder is needed in a circuit to make the lamp light.		
Plastic materials do not conduct electricity.		
The correct name for a single battery is a cell.		
Two wires are always needed in a circuit to light a lamp.		
A cell is what makes a circuit work.		
A connection point on a component is called a 'terminus'.		
Mains electricity can be very dangerous if it is misused.		
A mobile phone is operated by electricity.		
Electrical components must have two connection points.		
A switch is always needed to make a circuit work.		

Which two statements from the table do you think are most the important to remember when making a circuit?

_____

_____

> Compare your answers with a partner.
> Did you choose the same answers?

Activity 2: Light the lamp

Work with a partner to make a circuit to light the **lamp**. Choose which items from the list you are going to use. Draw your circuit in the space below. Label each component.

You will need
- a cell
- a lamp
- a crocodile lead
- a strip of aluminium
- a piece of string

  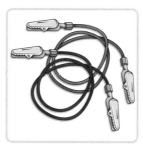  

Explain why you chose to use, or chose not to use, the string in your circuit.

_____

_____

Activity 3: Standard symbols

When Thomas Edison made the first commercially successful electric light bulb in 1879, he wanted to share his invention with other scientists. He drew the circuit to make his bulb work using symbols to represent the different parts. However, other scientists did not always know what his symbols represented. Over time, scientists began to use the same symbols until they became common across many different countries. Having symbols that are common across countries allows scientists to share their work easily. When symbols are commonly used and recognised by people around the world they become standard symbols.

Label the standard symbols below with what you think they represent.

buzzer	switch (open)	cell	wire	corners
motor	lamp	wire	switch (closed)	

_____   _____

_____   _____

_____   _____

_____   _____

Activity 4: Different circuits

Re-draw your circuit from activity 2 using standard symbols. Underneath, write two or three sentences to explain how your circuit works to light the lamp. Use the words in the box to help you.

cell	circuit	connection points
electrical conductor	electricity	flow

You will need
- a cell
- a motor
- a buzzer
- a switch
- a crocodile lead
- a strip of aluminium

Next, build a circuit using the items listed to make a motor spin. Draw your circuit using standard symbols.

Write sentences to explain how the motor is operated.
Use the words in the box to help you.

cell	electrical conductor
circuit	electricity
connection points	flow

_____

_____

_____

Finally, build a circuit that allows you to turn a buzzer on and off. Draw your circuit using standard symbols.

Write sentences to explain how the buzzer is operated.
Use the words in the box to help you.

cell	electrical conductor
circuit	electricity
connection points	flow

_____

_____

Key learning

In this lesson I have learned that: A simple **circuit** can be built with **electrical components** like a **cell**, an **electrical conductor** and a bulb, a **buzzer** or a **motor**. Electricity flows through a complete circuit. If there is a break between any of the **connection points**, the circuit won't work. A **switch** can be used to deliberately break the circuit. Scientists use standard symbols to represent electrical components in a circuit so that they can be recognised by others. It is important to choose the correct symbols when drawing a circuit, to use a ruler when drawing the wires and to make the circuit drawing a rectangular shape. There should be no gaps in the drawing of a circuit.

Homework

Look around your home and local area for symbols. Record the symbols and find out what they mean.

Key vocabulary

cell	dependent variable	independent variable
circuit	comparative test	lux

Activity 1: Using two or more cells

This is the symbol for two cells:

Work out and draw the symbol for three cells.

What are three important things to remember about drawing a circuit diagram?

_____

_____

Activity 2: Investigation questions

Scientists work by having an idea about something, then finding a way to test it. First, they must turn their idea into a question. Read the statements about making a lamp brighter. Turn them into questions that could be investigated. The first one has been done for you.

1. **If you have more lamps, they will be brighter.**

   Investigation question: How does the number of lamps affect the brightness of each lamp?

2. **If you have a bigger cell, the lamp will be brighter.**

   Investigation question: _____

3. **If you have thinner wires, the lamp will be brighter.**

   Investigation question: _____

4. **If you add a switch, the lamp will be brighter.**

   Investigation question: _____

5. **If you have more cells, the lamp will be brighter.**

   Investigation question: _____

Activity 3: How does the number of cells affect the brightness of the lamp?

You are going to gather evidence to answer the question: How does the number of cells affect the brightness of the lamp?

Build three different circuits using one, two and three cells. This inquiry is a comparative test because you are comparing three circuits.

The part of the circuit that you need to change in order to answer the question is called the independent variable.

The part of the circuit that you need to compare or measure is called the dependent variable.

Complete the sentences, then describe your test.

The independent variable in this test is the _____

The dependent variable in this test is the _____

Describe how you will compare the brightness of each lamp. The unit that the brightness of the lamp is measured in is lux (lx).

_____

_____

Draw the three circuits in the boxes. Remember to use the standard symbols. Record your results in the table.

Circuit	Number of cells	Brightness (lx)
1		
2		
3		

Circuit 1

Circuit 2

Circuit 3

Key learning

In this lesson I have learned that: A **circuit** is made up of **electrical components**. A battery provides electricity for the circuit, and we call a single battery a **cell**. More than one cell can be used in a circuit. If the circuit includes a lamp, we can use a light sensor on a data logger to measure light. Light is measured in **lux** (lx).The part of the circuit that is changed is called the **independent variable**. The part of the circuit that is measured is called the **dependent variable**. The more cells that a circuit has, the brighter the lamp will be.

Homework

Think of light sources that do not need electricity to work. Explain how these light sources were important before the invention of electricity.

Key vocabulary

cell   circuit   voltage   volts

Activity 1: Voltage in circuits

A cell is measured in voltage. Voltage is the measurement of the size of the push sending electricity around a circuit. It is measured in volts (V). Each cell in the diagram below has 1.5V.

Work out and write the voltage in each circuit.

A

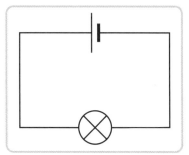

Voltage = _____

B

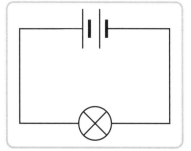

Voltage = _____

C

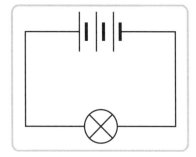

Voltage = _____

Using the diagrams A, B and C above and the learning from the last lesson, predict what you think will happen to the brightness of the bulb in each of the circuits.

A _____

B _____

C _____

These batteries all have a voltage of 1.5V.

Predict what you think would happen to the brightness of the bulb if you placed each battery in turn in the circuit in the last activity.

_____

_____

Tick (✓) the statement below that you are predicting here.

A. If you have more lamps, they will be brighter. ☐

B. If you have a bigger cell, the lamp will be brighter. ☐

C. If you have thinner wires, the lamp will be brighter. ☐

D. If you add a switch, the lamp will be brighter. ☐

E. If you have more cells, the lamp will be brighter. ☐

Does the size of the cell affect the brightness of the lamp? Tick one. Yes ☐ No ☐

Explain your answer below.

_____

_____

_____

_____

Activity 3: Comparative test: changing the brightness of a lamp

Choose one of the three remaining statements . Tick one (✓).

- If you have more lamps, they will be brighter. ☐
- If you have thinner wires, the lamp will be brighter. ☐
- If you add a switch, the lamp will be brighter. ☐

Make three circuits to test your question. Draw a circuit diagram for one and record the data.

You will need

- a cell (AA, 1.5V)
- a lamp (1.5V)
- four crocodile leads
- data logger or app to measure light

You can choose

- additional lamps
- fuse wires of different thicknesses
- switches
- extra crocodile leads

Drawing of circuit	Data

Result (answer to my question): _____

Variables changed: _____

Variables kept the same: _____

Key learning

In this lesson I have learned that: We know that a lamp will get brighter when more **cells** are added to a **circuit**. The size of the battery does not affect the brightness of the lamp if the voltage is the same. A cell is measured by its **voltage**. The unit of voltage is **volts**, which is shortened to V. Voltage is the measurement of the size of the push sending electricity around a circuit. We can compare different circuits to find the answer to a question. This is called a comparative enquiry.

Homework

Some electricity is generated by using fossil fuels. Find out what fossil fuels are used for and how they are damaging for the environment.

Lesson 4 How can we change how other components work?

Key vocabulary

cell circuit electrical component switch voltage

Activity 1: Increasing voltage: Test 1

You will need

- a cell
- a buzzer
- a switch
- crocodile leads

Draw a simple circuit with a cell, a switch and a buzzer. Mark the voltage on the diagram, then build the circuit. Predict what you think will happen to the buzzer when the voltage is increased and complete the sentence below.

I predict that when the voltage in the circuit is increased, the buzzer ____________________

____

Add another cell to your circuit. Listen to what happens to the sound of the buzzer. Draw the circuit diagram below and mark on the voltage. Complete the sentence below.

We found that when the voltage in the circuit was increased, the buzzer ____________________

____

Circle the answer that summarises your results: The evidence supports/refutes my prediction.

Activity 2: Increasing voltage: Test 2

> I predict that a motor will spin faster if the voltage in the circuit is increased.

You will need

- cells
- a motor
- crocodile leads
- a propeller
- a small ball of paper

Rewrite the prediction above as an investigation question.

_____

_____

_____

Build a circuit, then attach the propeller to the motor to act as a fan. This will blow the paper so you can test the speed of the motor as you add cells to the circuit. Work with a partner to gather evidence that will support or refute the prediction. You can:

- Bring the fan toward the paper ball and measure the distance at which the paper moves.
- Place the ball of paper the same distance from the fan and measure how far it is blown.

Decide which method you are going to use. Complete the heading in the table below and record your measurements.

Change the voltage in the circuit and record your results below. Take each measurement three times.

Voltage (V)	_____	_____	_____
1.5			
3			
4.5			

Draw the three circuits you built in the space below.

Conclusion

We found that when the voltage in the circuit was increased, the motor _____

_____

This meant that the piece of paper _____

_____

Circle the answer that summarises your results: The evidence supports/refutes the prediction.

Key learning

In this lesson I have learned that: Electricity can flow through a loop of **electrical components** and we call this a **circuit**. If there is a break in the circuit, for example if the **switch** is off, it will stop the flow of electricity. All circuits need a battery to work. A battery is made up of one or more cells. Most **cells** have a **voltage** of 1.5V. We can change the circuit by changing the components within it. Changing the voltage in a circuit affects how a motor, lamp or buzzer behaves.

Homework

Research different ways of generating electricity without using fossil fuels.

Key vocabulary

circuit   voltage

Activity 1: Brighter or dimmer?

Look at these circuits. Decide if the lamp is brighter in Circuit A or Circuit B. Complete the sentences.

A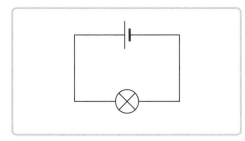

B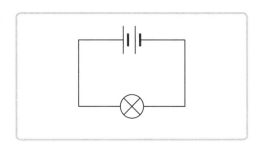

Both circuits have one lamp, but the voltage in Circuit _____ is _____

whereas the voltage in Circuit _____ is _____. Therefore, the lamp in

Circuit _____ will be brighter.

Activity 2: Brighter and dimmer circuits

Complete the sentence to explain which circuit of each pair will make the lamp shine the brightest and why.

1. A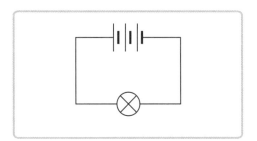

B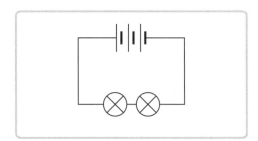

The lamps in Circuit _____ will be brighter. This is because _____

_____

2. A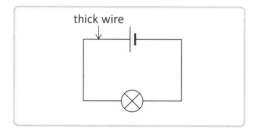
B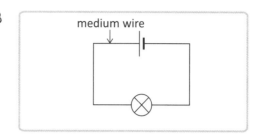

The lamp in Circuit _____ will be brighter. This is because _____

_____

3. A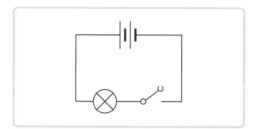
B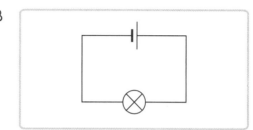

The lamp in Circuit _____ will be brighter. This is because _____

_____

4. A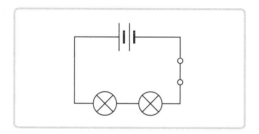
B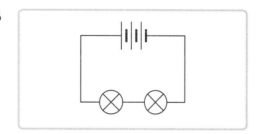

The lamp in Circuit _____ will be brighter. This is because _____

_____

Homework

Print or draw lots of different circuits on a piece of paper and cut them out. Play a game with someone at home by dealing out the cards so you each have the same number of cards. Then place your cards face down on the table. Turn over the top card and compare the circuits. The person whose circuit would have the brighter lamp wins both cards. If the circuits are the same, set the cards aside and turn over more cards. The person who runs out of cards first loses.

Body health

Lesson 1 How do we make healthy food choices?

Key vocabulary

carbohydrate	fibre	nutrient	salt
fats	mineral	protein	vitamin

Activity 1: Food groups

Can you remember why each food group is good for our bodies? Draw lines to link each food group to its description and then to the examples.

Carbohydrates	Helps our bodies to grow and repair	eggs, nuts, fish, meat, legumes, seeds
Proteins	Helps food to move easily through our digestive system	potatoes, rice, pasta, lentils, sweet potatoes
Fats	Give us energy	fruits, vegetables, milk, fish, meat, nuts
Fibre (roughage)	Give us energy and helps build our bodies	sweets, sugary drinks, desserts, snacks
Vitamins and minerals	Help our bodies to grow, function and repair	processed foods such as crisps and ready meals
Sugar	a type of carbohydrate	fruit, vegetables, wholemeal bread, brown rice
Salt	a small amount prevents low blood pressure	cheese, cream, oils, nuts, oily fish

What can you remember about a balanced diet? Why is it a good idea to eat salt, sugar and fat in small amounts?

Activity 2: High-fibre snacks

Fibre helps our digestive system to work well so we don't get constipated. It also lowers our risk of getting some diseases. A food is classed as high fibre if it has 6g or more of fibre per 100g.

Look at these food labels and sort the snacks into groups of high fibre, medium fibre and low fibre. You could colour-code them or mark them each with a letter. Use the information to recommend a high-fibre snack to someone who needs to eat more fibre.

Carrot sticks

	per 100 g
Protein	100 g
Carbohydrate	10 g
Fats	0.2 g
Fibre	2.8 g
Sodium/salt	0.069 g

Hummus

	per 100 g
Protein	6.8 g
Carbohydrate	10.6 g
Fats	25.4 g
Fibre	3.4 g
Sodium/salt	0.61 g

Potato crisps

	per 100 g
Protein	0.7 g
Carbohydrate	55 g
Fats	30 g
Fibre	3.9 g
Sodium/salt	1.5 g

Dried apricots

	per 100 g
Protein	2.7 g
Carbohydrate	49.2 g
Fats less than	0.5 g
Fibre	9.5 g
Sodium/salt less than	0.001 g

Salted peanuts

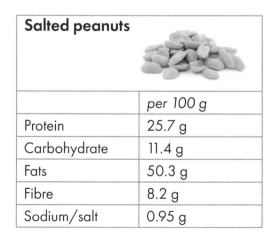

	per 100 g
Protein	25.7 g
Carbohydrate	11.4 g
Fats	50.3 g
Fibre	8.2 g
Sodium/salt	0.95 g

Halloumi cheese

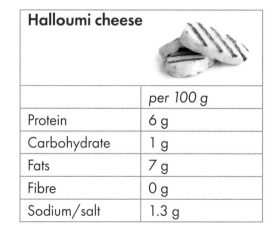

	per 100 g
Protein	6 g
Carbohydrate	1 g
Fats	7 g
Fibre	0 g
Sodium/salt	1.3 g

Bananas

	per 100 g
Protein	1.1 g
Carbohydrate	23 g
Fats	0.3 g
Fibre	2.6 g
Sodium/salt	0.001 g

Plain popcorn

	per 100 g
Protein	13 g
Carbohydrate	78 g
Fats	5 g
Fibre	14.5 g
Sodium/salt	0.008 g

Vegatable pakora

	per 100 g
Protein	7.3 g
Carbohydrate	25.1 g
Fats	20.6 g
Fibre	5.9 g
Sodium/salt	0.27 g

Rice crackers

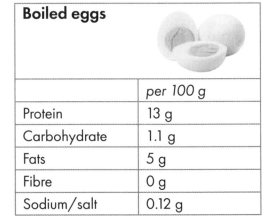

	per 100 g
Protein	9.1 g
Carbohydrate	78.4 g
Fats	6.8 g
Fibre	3.4 g
Sodium/salt	4.25 g

Chocolate digestives

	per 100 g
Protein	6.7 g
Carbohydrate	62.5 g
Fats	23.6 g
Fibre	3 g
Sodium/salt	0.94 g

Boiled eggs

	per 100 g
Protein	13 g
Carbohydrate	1.1 g
Fats	5 g
Fibre	0 g
Sodium/salt	0.12 g

Key learning

In this lesson I have learned that: Our bodies need a wide range of **nutrients** to stay healthy. We can get these nutrients by eating food from different food groups, such as **carbohydrates**, **proteins**, **fats** and **fibre**. We also need a variety of **vitamins** and **minerals**.

Homework

Interview a family member about how the food they eat has changed over their lifetime. Ask them if there are any foods that they eat now that they didn't eat when they were younger. Ask them if they think their diet is more or less healthy nowadays. Ask them to explain their answer.

Key vocabulary

| healthy | malnutrition | mineral | nutrient | vitamin |

Activity 1: Healthy foods

Draw pictures or write the names of four different healthy snacks in the boxes. Around each snack add information to explain which food group or groups it comes from and what nutrients it provides to your body.

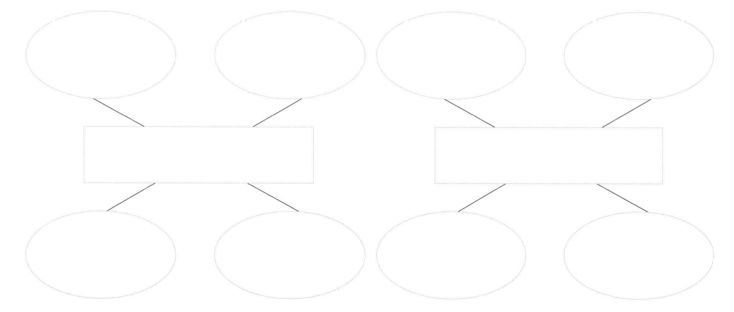

Activity 2: James Lind

You will need

- secondary sources about James Lind
- secondary sources about sailors in the 1700s

Read the information about James Lind and answer the questions on the next page.

Over 250 years ago, James Lind was a doctor on a sailing ship. He noticed that lots of the crew were ill. They had a disease called scurvy. James Lind noticed that the sailors' diet was very poor. They mainly ate salt beef and biscuits. He wanted to know if there was something missing from the sailors' diet. He got 12 sailors and fed them all something different. After a while, the sailors who ate oranges and lemons got better. James Lind proved that vitamin C cures scurvy.

James Lind

How did James Lind carry out his comparative test?

What was the variable that he changed?

What did he measure?

Carry out research about James Lind using the sources you have gathered. Make notes, then use the grid below to plan a four-part freeze-frame drama sequence to tell others:

- what James Lind did
- what he found out
- how it affected what we know today.

Key learning

In this lesson I have learned that: We need to have a balanced diet in order for our bodies get the right amount of **nutrients** to be **healthy** and work properly. If someone is over- or under-nourished, they are suffering with **malnutrition**. This means their body does not have the right balance of **vitamins** and minerals.

Homework

Think about four popular foods that are low in nutrients. Create a menu of food swaps for each food to help people improve their nutrition.

Key vocabulary

arteries   heart rate   oxygen   pulse   veins

Activity 1: Timing your heart rate

Carry out one of the activities below for two minutes and record your pulse rate straight afterwards. Then record your pulse rate again one minute later, then again at five-minute intervals afterwards.

You will need
- a stopwatch
- a pulse meter or smartwatch

March quickly on the spot. Lift your knees high and swing your arms.

Why do our hearts need exercise?

Do squats or lunges. If you are doing lunges, remember to change legs.

Time	Pulse rate			
0 min	A	At rest	(bpm)	
2 min	B	Straight after physical activity	(bpm)	
3 min	C	After 1 minute	(bpm)	
7 min	D	After 5 minutes	(bpm)	
12 min	E	After 10 minutes	(bpm)	
17 min	F	After 15 minutes	(bpm)	

Activity 2: Heart rate line graph

Plot your results as a line graph.

Graph title: _____

_____

This graph is to record: _____

_____

_____

_____

_____

_____

_____

Work out your recovery rate. Subtract your pulse rate one minute after physical activity from your pulse rate straight after physical activity. The larger the number, the better your recovery rate is. You can improve your recovery rate by being more physically active.

Pulse rate B	–	Pulse rate C	=	Recovery rate

Key learning

In this lesson I have learned that: Your heart pumps blood around the body, delivering **oxygen**, nutrients and water. Blood travels through **arteries** and **veins**, and your heart can beat up to 100,000 times a day. If you rest a finger on an artery, you might be able to feel your **pulse**, which is the movement of blood as it is pushed by the heart. You can work out your **heart rate** by feeling your pulse.

Homework

Create a game to get your family or friends active. Write an explanation of how it gets people moving.

Key vocabulary

chemicals   lungs

Activity 1: Smoking and vaping

What effects can smoking and vaping have on the body? Read each statement and write it in the correct place in the Venn diagram.

Causes yellow fingers and teeth

Contains tar which damages the lungs

Causes inflammation of the lungs

Makes asthma attacks more likely

Raises blood pressure

Contains cancer-causing chemicals

Causes dry mouth and throat

Causes 'popcorn lung'

Affects bone health

Contains nicotine

Affects the health of teeth and gums and can cause tooth loss

Causes heart disease

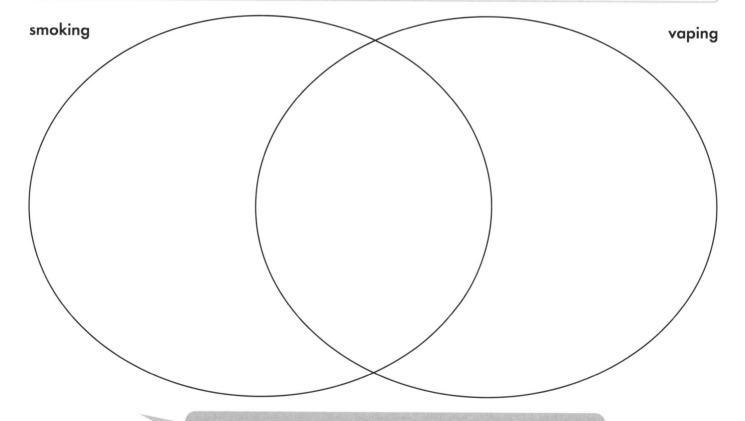

smoking   **vaping**

Do you know any other side effects of smoking or vaping?

Read the Smoking and Vaping Factsheet below and add more information to the venn diagram.

SMOKING AND VAPING FACTSHEET

What does smoking do to your lungs?

Smoking reduces your lung capacity – the amount of air you can breathe in.

Tobacco smoke contains lots of chemicals that are bad for our bodies and cause illness. Chemicals such as acrolein, formaldehyde, nitrogen oxide and cadmium.

Tobacco smoke contains a gas called carbon monoxide, a poisonous gas that is harmful to human health when inhaled.

What does vaping do to your lungs?

Vaping involves heating a liquid and inhaling the vapour into the lungs. Over time, vaping can lead to lung damage. This condition is known as 'popcorn lung'.

Vapes do not contain tobacco, but are harmful to health and are not safe. Scientists are still exploring the long-term risks of vaping.

What does nicotine do to the body?

Cigarettes and vapes both contain nicotine. Nicotine is a drug that changes the chemistry in your brain and affects how the body works. It increases your blood pressure breathing and heart rate. Nicotine is addictive. When people are addicted to nicotine, they become irritable without it, so they crave more and more.

There is usually less nicotine in a vape than in a cigarette.

Did you know?

- Tobacco kills more than 8 million people each year.
- Both smoking and vaping can irritate the lungs and make asthma attacks more likely.

Short- and long-term effects of smoking

Short-term: smelly clothes, hair and breath, stained fingers and teeth, coughing, increased heart rate and high blood pressure.

Longer-term: lung damage, lung cancer, heart damage, cancer of the mouth, throat and lips, pregnancy complications, smoking makes you appear much older, passive smoking can cause asthma and cancer.

Activity 2: Smoking advice

Read this letter from a young girl who has recently felt forced to try smoking. Talk to a partner or small group about how it would feel if it were you and what advice you would give her to explain the risks associated with smoking.

Dear Cyber Aunt Asma,

My name is Yasmin and I am 11 years old. I have recently started secondary school.

On the way home from school, I usually go to the park with my friends, but recently my friend sneaked out some cigarettes and a lighter from her older sister's handbag. Then she lit up and smoked in front of me and my other close friends. She called me names, saying I was a wimp for not trying it. This made me feel low and depressed, as I don't like being called names, and we have known each other for such a long time.

So, one day, just to shut her up, I tried just one puff. I hated it. I felt so disappointed with myself and I knew I shouldn't have done it. The next day, I spoke to my form tutor because I could hardly sleep. She talked to me about peer pressure and standing up for myself, but now I am thinking of every excuse I can to avoid going to the park with my friend again. And she has started hanging around with some other, older girls.

Please help, I feel so lonely and I don't know who to talk to.

Yasmin

Plan a reply to her letter. Think about the scientific facts you could use about smoking, to help her stand up to her friends.

Dear Yasmin,

Thank you for your letter. I'm sorry you are feeling lonely. Smoking is _____

_____

_____

_____

_____

_____

_____

_____

_____

_____

_____

_____

_____

_____

_____

_____

_____

_____

_____

Key learning

Some people choose to smoke tobacco through cigarettes, cigars or pipes. Tobacco contains various toxic **chemicals** that can be bad for the **lungs**. Vapes can be used to help someone give up smoking, but vapes can also cause damage to our lungs.

Homework

Write a script for a public health TV advert about smoking or vaping. Explain why it is bad for you.

William Collins' dream of knowledge for all began with the publication of his first book in 1819.
A self-educated mill worker, he not only enriched millions of lives, but also founded a flourishing publishing house. Today, staying true to this spirit, Collins books are packed with inspiration, innovation and practical expertise.
They place you at the centre of a world of possibility and give you exactly what you need to explore it.

Published by Collins
An imprint of HarperCollins*Publishers*
The News Building, 1 London Bridge Street, London, SE1 9GF, UK

HarperCollins*Publishers*
Macken House, 39/40 Mayor Street Upper, Dublin 1, D01 C9W8, Ireland

Browse the complete Collins catalogue at
collins.co.uk

British Library Cataloguing-in-Publication Data
A catalogue record for this publication is available from the British Library.

Development Editor: Kathryn Kendall Boucher
Series Editor: Jane Turner
Consultant Reviewer: David Allen
Publisher: Laura White
Copyeditor: Sarah Snashall
Proofreader: Kariss Holgarth
Cover Designer: Amparo at Kneath Associates
Packager: Oriel Square
Typesetter: Tech-Set
Production Controller: Alhady Ali
Printed and bound in Great Britain by Martins the Printers

This book contains FSC™ certified paper and other controlled
sources to ensure responsible forest management.

For more information visit: www.harpercollins.co.uk/green

collins.co.uk/sustainability

Acknowledgements
This work is adapted from the original work, Snap Science Second Edition Year 6.
All images are from Shutterstock.

The publishers gratefully acknowledge the permission granted to reproduce the copyright material in this book. Every effort has been made
to trace copyright holders and to obtain their permission for the use of copyright material. The publishers will gladly receive any information
enabling them to rectify any error or omission at the first opportunity.